Tim Nowak

Why can the movie "8 Mile" be considered a local color story?

GRIN Verlag

Bibliografische Information der Deutschen Nationalbibliothek:

Die Deutsche Bibliothek verzeichnet diese Publikation in der Deutschen National-
bibliografie; detaillierte bibliografische Daten sind im Internet über http://dnb.d-
nb.de/ abrufbar.

Imprint:

Copyright © 2010 GRIN Verlag GmbH
Druck und Bindung: Books on Demand GmbH, Norderstedt Germany
ISBN: 978-3-640-82172-3

This book at GRIN:

http://www.grin.com/en/e-book/165699/why-can-the-movie-8-mile-be-considered-
a-local-color-story

GRIN - Your knowledge has value

Der GRIN Verlag publiziert seit 1998 wissenschaftliche Arbeiten von Studenten, Hochschullehrern und anderen Akademikern als eBook und gedrucktes Buch. Die Verlagswebsite www.grin.com ist die ideale Plattform zur Veröffentlichung von Hausarbeiten, Abschlussarbeiten, wissenschaftlichen Aufsätzen, Dissertationen und Fachbüchern.

Visit us on the internet:

http://www.grin.com/

http://www.facebook.com/grincom

http://www.twitter.com/grin_com

Table of contents

1 Definition: Local color

Local color or regional literature is fiction and poetry that focuses on the characters, dialect, customs, topography, and other features particular to a specific region. Influenced by Southwestern and Down East humor, between the Civil War and the end of the nineteenth century this mode of writing became dominant in American literature.[1]

Especially Representatives of the United States were for example Mark Twain and Mary Austin, Zone Gale, Hamlin Garland and - probably the most famous one - Bret Hart.

"The short story "The Outcasts of Poker Flat" is a superb example of local color fiction" because it has the following characteristics: a) it is written for popular fiction, b) it contains accurate dialect, c) it shows realistic representations of local customs, dress, mannerisms, and habits of thought, d) it contains sentimentality, e) it contains humor, f) it contains the subject of life, friendship, and love, g) it came from personal experience of the author, and h) it contains eccentric characters.[2]

"Local Color" has not only played a big role in the past but can be also found in the present. In the following we are going to find out if the movie "8 Mile" is a typical "Local Color" story. To begin with we will be looking at the most important information of the movie which includes a summary, a biography of the Producer and Director Curtis Hanson, a biography of Eminem and the most important figures. After that we are going to talk about three songs of the movie and finally we are going to see that the movie "8 Mile" has a lot of local color characteristics.

---

[1] Campbell, Donna M. "Regionalism and Local Color Fiction." 1865-1895. Athens: Ohio University Press, 1997. Web. 1 Nov. 2010 <http://wsu.edu/~campbelld/amlit/lcolor.html>.
[2] "Local Color Fiction." Example Essays. N.p., n.d. Web. 5 Oct. 2010. <http://www.exampleessays.com/viewpaper/66953.html>.

2 Why can the movie "8 Mile" be considered a local color story?

2.1 Important information about the movie

2.1.1 Summary of the movie "8 Mile"

Right after Jimmy ("B Rabbit") Smith (Eminem, Picture 1,2) and his girlfriend Janeane (Taryn Manning, Picture 3) had split up in 1995, the 23-old has to move back to his alcoholic, unemployed mother Stephanie (Kim Basinger, Picture 4). She lives with her little daughter Lily (Chloe Greenfield, also Picture 4) and her lover Greg Buehl (Michael Shannon, Picture 5) – a former school friend of her son – in a trailer easterly of a Road called 8 Mile in Detroit. The money, B Rabbit earns as an unskilled worker at an automobile factory is not even enough for the rent but his mother doesn't want to bother Greg being scared of losing this man. However, Stephanie's boyfriend finds the eviction proceedings on accident and leaves her.

Although B Rabbit is white, his Afro-American friend David ("Future") Porter (Mekhi Phifer, Picture 6) forces him to take part in Hip-Hop-Battles, which are presented by him in the eyesore "The Shelter". In every round two competitors meet and they both have 45 seconds time to make an off-cuff Rap song to insult each other. The participant who more enthusiastically the audience claps at moves up one round. Because of his stage fright B Rabbit vomits backstage before the rap battle. On his turn he is not able to say a word and the crowed boos him off the stage.

In spite of his fail Future does not give up on him and Eminem gets to know a new friend Alex (Brittany Murphy, Picture 7) who also believes in his exceptional gift as a Rapper. Alex dreams about a career as a model.

B Rabbit is scared off getting sneered at in "The Shelter" again and he is not sure if he should listen to Wink (Eugene Byrd, Picture 8), a guy who offers to record a demo with him boasting about popularizing him. Jealously B Rabbit is watching when Wink promises Alex to help her start a career as a model. After a fight with Future, B. Rabbit is left with no other choice than taking Wink's offer. But then he catches Alex and Wink having sex. Angrily he beats him up, however, later that day Wink comes back with his gang and beats up B Rabbit as payback.

After Alex reconciled with B Rabbit, she decides to move to New York for a better future.

B Rabbit also reconciled with Future and reports in "The Shelter again". Round to Round he works himself to the final of the rap battle where he meets the favorite "Papa Doc" (Anthony Mackie, Picture 9). As a result B Rabbit beats him and as a result he gains respect in the Detroit Hip-Hop-Scene which is mainly controlled by black people.[34]

2.1.2 Biography of the director and producer Curtis Hanson

Curtis Lee Hanson (Picture 10), born in Reno Nevada 1945, grew up in Los Angeles. When Hanson dropped out of high school he started to work as a photographer for "Cinema magazine" which his uncle owned. "After years of editing and taking photographs for Cinema magazine, Hanson turned to screenwriting and directing."[5] His career started with the movie "Sweet Kill" in 1973. The movie was not only written by Hanson but also directed and produced by him together with Roger Corman. After that he directed many other movies like "Losin' It" (1983), "The Children Of Times Square" (1986), "The Bedroom Window" (1987), "Bad Influence" (1990), "The Hand that Rocks the Cradle" (1992), "The River Wild" (1994), "L.A. Confidential" 1997, "Wonder Boys" (2000), "8 Mile" (2002), "In Her Shoes" (2005) and "Lucky You" (2007).[6] *"After receiving Best Screenplay Oscar from Walter Matthau and 'Jack Lemmon'"[7]* Hanson said: *"Being given this Award*

[3] "8 Mile (film)." Wikipedia. N.p., n.d. Web. 12 Oct. 2010.
<http://en.wikipedia.org/wiki/8_Mile_(film)#Plot>.
[4] Davis, Nicholas. "8 Mile." Nick's Flick Picks. Ed. Davis Nick. N.p., Nov. 2002. Web. 12 Oct. 2010.
<http://www.nicksflickpicks.com/8mile.html>.
[5] "Curtis Hanson biography." tribute.ca. N.p., n.d. Web. 2 Nov. 2010.
<http://www.tribute.ca/people/curtis-hanson/1739/>.
[6] "Curtis Hanson." Wikipedia. N.p., n.d. Web. 13 Oct. 2010.
<http://en.wikipedia.org/wiki/Curtis_Hanson>.

by two actors I will always associate with Billy Wilder makes it all the sweeter."[7] His philosophy about movies is that he wants:

> *"to allow people to think about the movie the way I always thought about movies I watched and admired. [...] When they're watching the movie I want them to watch the movie, not be distracted listening to me or other people."*[3]

2.1.2 Biography of Eminem

Marshall Bruce Mathers III (Picture 11) was born in St. Joseph, Missouri in 1972. The Rapper and Producer grew up in a predominant Afro-American residential area in Detroit. His dad left Eminem when he was only three months together with his mother who was 17 years old. She was addicted to drugs and violent. His only model, father substitute and friend was his uncle Ronnie who shot himself while a crime in 1991. In the year 1987 he recorded his first Demo tape which he used to be able to participate in the Detroit rap scene. Seven years later his girlfriend Kimberly Ann Scott who he married in 1999 gave birth to his daughter Hailie Jade Scott. While his first performances he called himself "M&M" (his initials) which he changed within the 1990s to "Eminem" spoken as "em 'n em". His first album "Infinite" turned out in 1996 and was not very popular. 1998 Dr. Dre (Andre Romell Young):

> *Singed Eminem to his Aftermath label after hearing the rapper free styling on a Los Angeles radio station. The Slim Shady LP was released on Feb. 23, 1999 and hit No. 2 on the Billboard charts within weeks. The Slim Shady LP was 3 times platinum.*[8]

The album "The Marshall Mathers LP" won 3 Grammies and *"was the first rap album ever to be nominated 'Album of the Year', selling more than 8 million records in the United States alone."*[8] Although Eminem was going through difficult times with his mother and with his wife - she sued him for ten million dollars compensation in each case - Eminem is with more than 65 Million sold albums considered as the most successful white Rapper worldwide.[8]

---

[7] "Curtis Hanson." IMDb. N.p., n.d. Web. 13 Oct. 2010.
<http://www.imdb.com/name/nm0000436/bio>.
[8] "Biography of Eminem." IMDb. N.p., n.d. Web. 15 Aug. 2010.
<http://www.imdb.com/name/nm0004896/bio>.

2.1.3 Central figures of the movie "8 Mile"

The white rapper Jimmy Smith Jr. (B. Rabbit, Picture 1 and Picture 2) played by Eminem (Picture 11) himself lives on the crime, unemployment and corruption side of the road "8 Mile" which separates the city center of Detroit. He works in a car factory but the money just lasts for his living. After breaking up with his pregnant girlfriend (Picture 3), he has to move back to his drug-addicted mother Stephanie (Kim Basinger, Picture 4), her boyfriend, a former school friend of Jimmy and his little sister Lily (Chloe Greenfield, also Picture 4) into a trailer. Becoming a professional rapper one day is his dream and his friend Future (Mekhi Phifer, Picture 6) who moderates freestyle battles in a club called "The Shelter", promotes B. Rabbit by giving him the chance to participate in rap battles but Jimmy blows his first opportunity because of stage fright. The talented Rapper finds Alex (Brittany Murphy, Picture 7), some kind of fellow sufferer who also wants to escape the ghettos of Detroit through artistic success. Alex believes in Jimmy but cheats on him to help herself starting a career as a model. B. Rabbit works hard to get his live straight and his friend future gives him another chance to battle in "The Shelter". Eminem is not afraid anymore and works his way up to the final where he beats his biggest opponent and wins the competition.

2.2 Music of the movie "8 Mile"

2.2.1 Interpretation of the song "Lose Yourself"

"Lose Yourself" is a hip hop song released in 2002 as part of the soundtrack to the movie "8 Mile". The song is 5 minutes and 20 seconds long, has three verses, a refrain and talks about the character B. Rabbit, played by Eminem, who has the potential to be a rapper but doesn't take the first opportunity to show everybody. Now he has to work even harder to show everyone what he is able to do. *"Reaching #1 in a 24 charts worldwide, "Lose Yourself" became a worldwide success. It spent 12 weeks atop the U.S. Billboard Hot 100, the longest-running #1 of 2002."* [9] Eminem's song was nominated and won an Academy Award Oscar for Best Original Song in 2002. "8 Mile" was the first movie to win an Academy award with a Hip-hop song. At the beginning of the song "Lose Yourself" which is based on the movie "8 Mile", Eminem talks about one opportunity the character Jimmy Smith, Jr. *"Look, if you had one shot, or one opportunity To seize everything you ever wanted-One moment Would you capture it or just let it slip?"* [10] has and asks the question if he took advantage of it. In the first verse he tells us that he is very nervous: *"His palms are sweaty, knees weak, arms are heavy - There's vomit on his sweater already, mom's spaghetti - He's nervous"* [7] and does not take that one opportunity because he keeps forgetting the words in front of the crowd he is trying to remember

> *but he keeps on forgettin what he wrote down,- the whole crowd goes so loud - He opens his mouth, but the words won't come out - He's choking now, everybody's joking now - The clock's run out, time's up over, bloah!* [7]

even though he looks fine and ready *"but on the surface he looks calm and ready to drop bombs"* [7]. In the following he raps about the fact that he is *"so mad"* [7] he didn't take the chance *"but he won't give up that – Easy, no "* [7] and work hard his way back – out of his situation - by practicing everywhere:

> *When he goes back to his mobile home, that's when it's – Back to the lab again [...]I was playing in the beginning, the mood all changed - I been chewed up and spit out and booed off stage - But I kept rhyming and stepwritin the next cypher* [7]

---

[9] "Lose Yourself." Wikipedia. N.p., n.d. Web. 16 Oct. 2010.
<http://en.wikipedia.org/wiki/Lose_Yourself>.
[10] "Eminem Lyrics." AZLyrics. N.p., n.d. Web. 20 Oct. 2010.
<http://www.azlyrics.com/lyrics/eminem/loseyourself.html>.

Both the second and third verse are based on Eminem's live. He stresses that by saying *"And it's no movie, there's no Mekhi Phifer, this is my live"[7]*. The main meaning of the last two verses is about Eminem's problem starting a career in the rap scene *"His hoes don't want him no more, he's cold product – They moved on to the next schmoe who flows – He nose dove and sold nada"[7]* and to take care of his daughter at the same time *"He's grown farther from home, he's no father – He goes home and barely knows his own daughter [...] And I can't provide the right type of life for my family"[7]*. Rap is also Eminem's only option *"Success is my only motherfucking option, failure's not"[7]*. According to Eminem the message of the song is to lose yourself - the meaning is already in the title - in the music, to remove every barrier, to ignore every interjection, blank out what everybody else criticizes, find yourself and your voice.

> *You better lose yourself in the music, the moment - You own it, you better never let it go - You only get one shot, do not miss your chance to blow - This opportunity comes once in a lifetime yo[7]*

At the end of the song Eminem finishes with the words: *"You can do anything you set your mind to, man"[711]*

2.2.2 Interpretation of the song "Juicy"

Another song in the movie "8 Mile" is called "Juicy", a hip hop song released in 1994 by *"The Notorious B.I. G."* (stage name), born in New York in 1977 with the Name Christopher George Latore Wallace. He was an American rapper who was shot in 1997 in Los Angeles.[12] In the movie the song starts with the chorus *"You know very well who you are - Don't let em hold you down, reach for the stars - You had a go, but not that many - 'cause you're the only one I'll give you good and plenty"[13]* and it is played when Eminem is together with his friends in the car doing silly things. The song is based on The Notorious B.I.G. and talks about the changes

---

[11] Mathers III, Marshall B., writ. Eminem - Lose Yourself Official Music Vi. Prod. Marshall B. Mathers III. 2003. Web. 20 Oct. 2010. <http://www.youtube.com/watch?v=H4JnoJ1W9fI>.
[12] "The Notorious B.I.G." Wikipedia. N.p., n.d. Web. 27 Oct. 2010. <http://en.wikipedia.org/wiki/The_Notorious_B.I.G.>.
[13] "Soundtrack - Notorious Big - Juicy." N.p., n.d. Web. 29 Oct. 2010. <http://lyricskeeper.de/de/soundtrack/notorious-big-juicy.html>.

that have been taken place since he has become a famous rapper. *"I made the change from a common thief - To up close and personal with robin leach"[7]*. Now he is rich and has a lot of money *"And I'm far from cheap, I smoke skunk with my peeps all day - Spread love, it's the brooklyn way"[7]*. He mentions that his dream became reality in all three verses.

> *"Now I'm in the limelight ' cause I rhyme tight [...] Born filla, the opposite of a winner [...] I never thought it could happen, this rappin' stuff [...]Now honies play me close like butter played toast [...]Sold out seats to hear biggie smalls speak – Livin' life without fear – Puttin' 5 karats in my baby girl's ears – Lunches, brunches, interviews by the pool [...] 50 inch screen, money green leather sofa – Got two rides, a limousine with a chauffeur – Phone bill about two g's flat – No need to worry, my accountant handles that"[7]*

Basically the content of the song is a *"rags-to-riches chronicle"[14]*, which isB. Rabbit's dream. In that scene you get exactly the feeling that is described through the song by The Notorious B.I.G., namely freedom, no fear and happiness. The song ends in the movie in the third verse with the words *"No Heat"[7]*, when the siren of a police car turned on and Jimmy gets pulled back to reality and fear.[15][16]

2.2.3 Interpretation of the song "Get Money"

Another song by The Notorious B.I.G. and Lil' Kim (Kimberly Denise Jones) - born in New York in 1975[17] - called "Get Money" is played in the movie right after a rap-battle scene. The song fits perfectly in with the title "Get Money" because B. Rabbit is sitting in his car with his friends talking about becoming famous and "getting Money" one day.[18]

---

[14] Huey, Steve. "Ready to Die Review." allmusic. N.p., n.d. Web. 29 Oct. 2010.
<http://www.allmusic.com/album/ready-to-die-r203800/review>.
[15] "Juicy (The Notorious B.I.G. song)." Wikipedia. N.p., n.d. Web. 30 Oct. 2010.
<http://en.wikipedia.org/wiki/Juicy_(The_Notorious_B.I.G._song)#cite_note-1>.
[16] Wallace, Christopher G., writ. Biggie smalls - juicy. Prod. Christopher G. Wallace. 1994.
Christopher George Latore Wallace, 1994. Web. 5 Nov. 2010.
<http://www.youtube.com/watch?v=OsT8FaZnzdE>.
[17] "Lil' Kim." Wikipedia. N.p., n.d. Web. 30 Oct. 2010. <http://en.wikipedia.org/wiki/Lil'_Kim>.
[18] Jones, Kimberly D., and Clark Kent, writ. Junior M.A.F.I.A. feat. Notorious B.I.G.. Perf.
Christopher G. Wallace and Kimberly D. Jones. 1996. 1996. Web. 5 Oct. 2010.
<http://www.youtube.com/watch?v=etMpCz8eql8>.

2.3 Examination of local color characteristics

2.3.1 The movie "8 Mile"

The first local color characteristic we are going to have a look at is at the very beginning of the movie when Jimmy Smith Jr. is in a club called "The Shelter". All of the people around "Rabbit" are dark skin colored which is very typical for the rap scene in Detroit. In his first rap battle his opponent (also dark skinned) makes fun of him being white and that he *"shouldn't fight with the tight"*[19] He also tells him that he does not belong here ("The Shelter") because he is not black and he should go to the other white people: *"Cause this is Detroit - 60 Mile Road is that away"*[19]. After his friend Future announces Jimmy, he gets booed off stage before he even starts rapping because everybody has the prejudice that a "white one" can't rap.

If we talk about telling names in the movie, Jimmy's friend's name Future is very interesting because B. Rabbit depends on him to start a career or gain respect in the Detroit rap scene, so Future is his "future". His other friend called Wink has also a message. To wink at somebody is a sing of trust but in the movie Wink blows it when he cheats on Jimmy with his girlfriend.

Later when he takes the bus home, an older, black man keeps looking at him like he does not belong in this district of Detroit. Another scene where you can see only dark skinned people is at the car factory Jimmy works for. Originally black people moved to Detroit while World War II to work in War factories.[20]

"8 Mile" contains a lot of humor, too: Especially while rap battles when they make fun of each other. For example at the end of the movie Jimmy shows his butt to everybody or just about every rhyme they rap.

---

[19] Hanson, Curtis, dir. 8 Mile. Prod. Curtis Hanson. 2002. Universal Pictures. DVD-ROM.
[20] "Detroit Race Riot (1943)." Wikipedia. N.p., n.d. Web. 1 Nov. 2010.
<http://en.wikipedia.org/wiki/Detroit_Race_Riot_(1943)>.

The automobile industry is very typical for Detroit. Big companies like *"General Motors, Chrysler and American Motors"*[21] are in Detroit since Henry Ford built the first automobile industry in 1899 (also the "end" of local color stories).

When Jimmy takes the bus to work you can see what is typical for Detroit: Old and dilapidated buildings, the streets are not very clean, a gun shop which is a sign of high murder rate. According to the crime statistics on Wikipedia Detroit has the greatest murder rate in the whole country.[22] There are also a lot of violent scenes in the movie. For example: Jimmy and his friends are shooting with a paint ball gun at a police car, they are smoking weed in the car, they burn a house after making party in it, when they have a fight with another group or when Jimmy gets beat up by his own friend Wink and his gang.

In Jimmy's gang is only one other white guy who shoots himself in his leg while a fight. The gun is his mom's because she is probably also white and scared of black people, so she wants to defend herself. When they want to visit him at his mom's home, you can see that he lives in an actual house that is clean and looks "welcome and worm". So there is a big difference and tension of white and black people in Detroit which is also very typical for this city.

A further aspect of local color characteristics is that the language has a certain touch of Detroit slang. They are always adding a "man", "you know", "Its all good in the hood", "What up doh" (for "what up dog"), "yeah", "my bad man", "big time", "whats up with you an Wink", "alright", "yo", "peace out", also a lot of violent words like "ass", "shit", "fuck", "fagit", "dog", "baby", "don't play me fuking stupid", "I don't give a shit", "I really fukin don't", "god damn", "spin that shit" etc. and at the beginning or at the end of a conversation they also shake hands in a certain style which is a sing of trust and friendship and also very typical in the Detroit scene.

---

[21] "History of Detroit." Wikipedia. N.p., n.d. Web. 1 Nov. 2010.
<http://en.wikipedia.org/wiki/History_of_Detroit>.
[22] "United States cities by crime rate." Wikipedia. N.p., n.d. Web. 1 Nov. 2010.
<http://en.wikipedia.org/wiki/United_States_cities_by_crime_rate>.

Another necessary aspect we need to be looking at is the clothes (costumes) everybody is wearing. Typical are non-expensive, old, casual wear like long sweaters or jogging pants.

The movie also contains the subject of life, friendship and love. Eminem's live, the strong friendship of Jimmy and Future and love (Jimmy's ex-girlfriend and a relationship with Alex). Future signs Jimmy up for another rap battle even he doesn't want him to. He knows that his friend is really good in rapping and wants to help him life a better live and maybe make his hobby (rapping) to his living on day. Jimmy gets mad at him at first but after a while he apologizes for it and later everything works out and they stick together (strong friendship). When Jimmy broke up with his pregnant girlfriend, we can see another typical problem in Detroit: Contraception.

Furthermore the last local color characteristic we are looking at in the movie is that the story is based – in this case – on Eminem's live. This represents only one person out of a lot like Dr. Dre, D12, Obie Trice, Paradime, Quest M.C.O.D.Y., Black Milk, Guilty Simpson, Apollo Brown, Fat Killaz, Chief, and Street Justice Crown Nation who escaped the ghettos through artistic success.[19]

3   Local color in Bavaria

In conclusion I believe that the movie "8 Mile" can be considered a local color story because it contains lots of local color characteristics like telling names, accurate dialect, humor, it shows realistic representations of local clothes, mannerisms and habits of thoughts, the subject of life, friendship, and love, and it is based – in this case – on Eminem's live. That means we still own local color in our society even not realizing it. For example in Bavaria: The "Oktoberfest" in Munich, "Lederhosen" and "Dirndl", "Trachtenvereine", "Maibaum", "Blasmusik", Bavarian dialect etc. which is an important part of our life and has to be cultivated in order to keep them alive.

Work consulted

Primary literature:

Hanson, Curtis, dir. 8 Mile. Prod. Curtis Hanson. 2002. Universal Pictures. DVD-
ROM.

Secondary literature:

Campbell, Donna M. "Regionalism and Local Color Fiction." 1865-1895.
Athens: Ohio University Press, 1997. Web. 1 Nov. 2010
<http://wsu.edu/~campbelld/amlit/lcolor.html>.

Davis, Nicholas. "8 Mile." Nick's Flick Picks. Ed. Davis Nick. N.p., Nov. 2002.
Web. 12 Oct. 2010.
<http://www.nicksflickpicks.com/8mile.html>.

Huey, Steve. "Ready to Die Review." allmusic. N.p., n.d. Web. 29 Oct. 2010.
<http://www.allmusic.com/album/ready-to-die-r203800/review>.

Jones, Kimberly D., and Clark Kent, writ. Junior M.A.F.I.A. feat. Notorious B.I.G..
Perf. Christopher G. Wallace and Kimberly D. Jones. 1996. 1996. Web. 5
Oct. 2010. <http://www.youtube.com/watch?v=etMpCz8eql8>.

Mathers III, Marshall B., writ. Eminem - Lose Yourself Official Music Vi. Prod.
Marshall B. Mathers III. 2003. Web. 20 Oct. 2010.
<http://www.youtube.com/watch?v=H4JnoJ1W9fI>.

Wallace, Christopher G., writ. Biggie smalls - juicy. Prod. Christopher G. Wallace.
1994. Christopher George Latore Wallace, 1994. Web. 3 Nov. 2010.
<http://www.youtube.com/watch?v=OsT8FaZnzdE>.

"Biography of Eminem." IMDb. N.p., n.d. Web. 15 Aug. 2010.
<http://www.imdb.com/name/nm0004896/bio>.

"Curtis Hanson." IMDb. N.p., n.d. Web. 13 Oct. 2010.
<http://www.imdb.com/name/nm0000436/bio>.

"Curtis Hanson." Wikipedia. N.p., n.d. Web. 13 Oct. 2010.
<http://en.wikipedia.org/wiki/Curtis_Hanson>.

"Curtis Hanson biography." tribute.ca. N.p., n.d. Web. 2 Nov. 2010.
<http://www.tribute.ca/people/curtis-hanson/1739/>.

"Detroit Race Riot (1943)." Wikipedia. N.p., n.d. Web. 1 Nov. 2010.
<http://en.wikipedia.org/wiki/Detroit_Race_Riot_(1943)>.

"Eminem Lyrics." AZLyrics. N.p., n.d. Web. 20 Oct. 2010.
     <http://www.azlyrics.com/lyrics/eminem/loseyourself.html>.

"History of Detroit." Wikipedia. N.p., n.d. Web. 1 Nov. 2010.
     <http://en.wikipedia.org/wiki/History_of_Detroit>.

"Juicy (The Notorious B.I.G. song)." Wikipedia. N.p., n.d. Web. 30 Oct. 2010.
     <http://en.wikipedia.org/wiki/Juicy_(The_Notorious_B.I.G._song)>.

"Lil' Kim." Wikipedia. N.p., n.d. Web. 30 Oct. 2010.
     <http://en.wikipedia.org/wiki/Lil'_Kim>.

"Local Color Fiction." Example Essays. N.p., n.d. Web. 5 Oct. 2010.
     <http://www.exampleessays.com/viewpaper/66953.html>.

"Lose Yourself." Wikipedia. N.p., n.d. Web. 16 Oct. 2010.
     <http://en.wikipedia.org/wiki/Lose_Yourself>.

"Soundtrack - Notorious Big - Juicy." N.p., n.d. Web. 29 Oct. 2010.
     <http://lyricskeeper.de/de/soundtrack/notorious-big-juicy.html>.

"The Notorious B.I.G." Wikipedia. N.p., n.d. Web. 27 Oct. 2010.
     <http://en.wikipedia.org/wiki/The_Notorious_B.I.G.>.

"United States cities by crime rate." Wikipedia. N.p., n.d. Web. 1 Nov. 2010.
     <http://en.wikipedia.org/wiki/United_States_cities_by_crime_rate>.

"8 Mile (film)." Wikipedia. N.p., n.d. Web. 12 Oct. 2010.
     <http://en.wikipedia.org/wiki/8_Mile_(film)#Plot>.

Pictures

Picture 1: The cover of the movie "8 Mile"

(http://www.eminem.net/8mile/images/8_mile_dvd_cover_front.jpg)

Picture 2: Jimmy Smith Jr.

(http://emgirl.homepage24.de/bilder/8mile115.jpg)

Picture 3: Jimmy's exgirlfriend Janeane

(http://www.laut.de/bilder/wortlaut/artists/b/boomkat/defimage1.jpg)

Picture 4: Jimmy's mom Stephanie
and her daughter Lily

(http://hollywoodjesus.com/movie/8_mile/34.jpeg)

Picture 5: Stephanie's boyfriend

(http://thumbnails.truveo.com/0023/21/D9/21D975E
2A7CFF5C5270BBB.jpg)

Picture 6: Jimmy's friend Future

(http://hollywoodjesus.com/movie/8_mile/33.jpeg)

Picture 7: Jimmy's girlfriend Alex

(http://www.eminem.net/8mile/images/brittany_mur
phy_8_mile.jpg)

Picture 8: Wink

(http://cdn5.movieclips.com/universal/8/8-mile-
2002/0005918_1867_MC_T.jpg)

Picture 9: "Papa Doc" and Jimmy

(http://i4.ytimg.com/vi/_aamQEHfZRM/default.jpg)

Picture 10: Curtis Hanson

(http://www.vootar.com/imgs/elementos/124404883
0_Curtis%20Hanson)

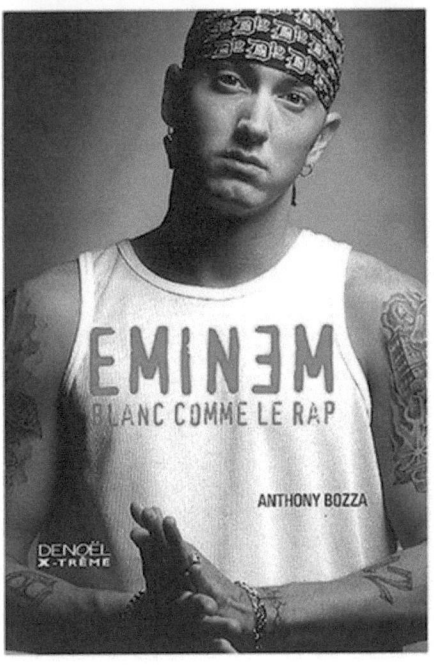

Picture 11: Eminem

(http://images-
eu.amazon.com/images/P/2207256030.08.LZZZZZZZ.j
pg)